Marcus Allen

By

Jane Mersky Leder

Edited By

Dr. Howard Schroeder

Professor in Reading and Language Arts
Dept. of Elementary Education
Mankato State University

Produced & Designed By

Baker Street Productions, Ltd.

CRESTWOOD HOUSE

Mankato, Minnesota
U.S.A.

LIBRARY OF CONGRESS CATALOGING IN PUBLICATION DATA

Leder, Jane Mersky.
Marcus Allen.

SUMMARY: A brief biography of the star running back of the Los Angeles Raiders football team.
1. Allen, Marcus, 1960-   —Juvenile literature. 2. Football players—United States—Biography—Juvenile literature. 3. National Football League—Juvenile literature. [1. Allen, Marcus, 1960-   . 2. Football players. 3. Afro-Americans—Biography] I. Schroeder, Howard. II. Baker Street Productions. III. Title.
GV939.A54L43   1985   796.332'092'4   [B]   [92]   84-11375
ISBN 0-89686-251-8

International Standard
Book Number:
0-89686-251-8

Library of Congress
Catalog Card Number:
84-11375

PHOTO CREDITS

Cover: Focus on Sports
Sports Illustrated: (Tony Tomsic) 4; (Richard Mackson) 17; (Heinz Kluetmeier) 40; (Ronald C. Modra) 41, 44
Wide World: 9, 10, 11, 13, 15, 23, 26-27, 36, 38-39, 47
United Press: 18, 35, 42-43
Focus on Sports: 20, 21, 24, 28, 31, 32, 37

Hwy. 66 South, Box 3427
Mankato, MN 56002-3427

TABLE
OF
CONTENTS

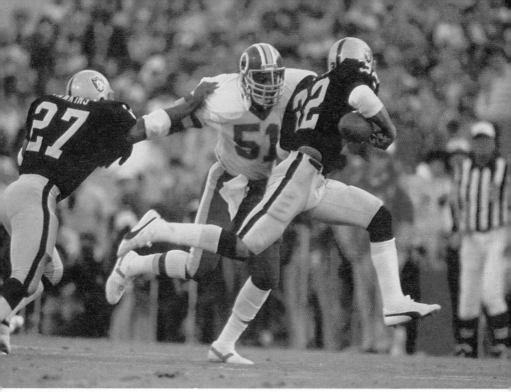

Marcus Allen on his way to a big gain in Super Bowl XVIII.

INTRODUCTION

He takes the football from the quarterback and tucks it under his arm. Running quickly forward, he slants to the sideline, gaining yards with long strides. Just when it looks like he is about to be tackled, the runner cuts back toward the center of the field. No one can catch him now. Marcus Allen is on his way to scoring another touchdown.

Marcus Allen likes to score touchdowns and likes to win. He started playing football at the age of ten. Since then, he has never been on a losing team. "I hate to lose," says Allen. "I just feel terrible inside when I lose." Allen always tries to play well. People expect that from him. But no one expects more from Allen than he himself. Allen is never content with what he does. He always wants to do better. Marcus dreams big, and lives his dreams.

GROWING UP IN SAN DIEGO

Marcus LaMarr Allen was born in San Diego, California on March 26, 1960. He was the second of six children. The Allens were a very close family. They spent a lot of time together. Marcus' dad, "Red," saw to that. His idea of child-raising was to keep Marcus and the other children very busy. That way, they wouldn't have time to get into trouble.

Marcus could be stubborn. Once the manager of his little league baseball team said he had to play shortstop instead of center field. Marcus only wanted to play center field. So, he called a strike. The manager of the team was "Red" Allen, his father!

There was a wall plaque in the den of the Allen home. It read:

Be careful of the words you say
So keep them soft and sweet
You never know from day to day
Which ones you'll have to eat.

Marcus learned a lesson from that wall plaque. He learned that what he said, and how he said it, could make a big difference. Marcus grew up respecting people and respecting himself.

Marcus also grew up with a strong belief in God. "God has blessed me," said Marcus. "And that is more important than anything. I really feel that everything I have done is because of Him. I feel He is guiding my life." Marcus' strong faith helped him stay away from alcohol and drugs. He had no interest in those things. "I saw too many people having their careers and families destroyed," he said.

Marcus attended Lincoln High in San Diego, California. He was an all-around athlete. Football was not his only sport. Marcus won letters in basketball, football, baseball, and track. He earned All-City and All-League honors as a guard in basketball. He played five different positions in baseball! His mother, Gwen, thought baseball was his best sport. She claimed he could have been as good as Brooks Robinson.

Marcus played linebacker and defensive back on the Lincoln High football team. In one game, he made thirty tackles. Lincoln's coach, Vic Player, forced Marcus to play quarterback his senior year. But Marcus was not happy with the change. He just wanted to be one of the boys. He did not want to be the head of the team.

Marcus decided to rebel against being the quarterback. One day during practice, he kept fumbling the snap from the center. Coach Player was hopping mad. He kicked Marcus off the team. "Get out of here," Player screamed. "And don't come back."

The next day Marcus returned to practice. He was very sorry for what he had done. He apologized over and over. Coach Player accepted his apologies. "If he hadn't come back," Player said, "I would have gone to him and begged. But Marcus will never believe that."

As it turned out, Lincoln went on to a 12-0-1 record that year with Marcus as quarterback. He passed for 1,900 yards and 18 touchdowns. His team won the San Diego County championship. Marcus rushed nine times for 197 yards in the championship game. He intercepted a pass and scored all five of his team's touchdowns. Marcus was the star of his team, and probably the best athlete to ever grow up in San Diego.

UNIVERSITY OF SOUTHERN CALIFORNIA

Almost every college in the country wanted Marcus on its football team. Oklahoma, for example, wanted him as a quarterback. The University of Southern California

(USC) wanted him as a defensive back. Marcus decided to stay in his home state and go to USC.

On the fourth day of football practice during his freshman year, USC's coach, John Robinson, suggested that Marcus try playing tailback. Unfortunately for Marcus, Charles White was already USC's first-string tailback. White was an excellent player. In fact, he won the Heisman Trophy in 1979, as the best college player in the country. So, Marcus spent most of his freshman year sitting on the bench.

The next spring, Coach Robinson asked Marcus if he would like to play fullback. There is no more unpleasant job at USC than playing that position. The fullback blocks, and then he blocks some more. When Marcus didn't accept Robinson's offer right away, the coach gave him some good advice. "Think about it, Marcus," he said. "You're not going to play much at tailback."

So Marcus agreed to move to fullback. He played poorly in spring practice. In the fall, he broke his nose while making a crushing block. But Marcus' broken nose did not stop him from playing football. By the end of the 1979 season, Marcus had become an excellent fullback. He was so good that he worried about having to play that position for the rest of his college career. Coach Robinson came up to him late in the season. "Marcus, you sacrificed for the good of the team," said the coach. "Yeah," answered Marcus, "I sacrificed my entire body!"

Marcus' sacrifice paid off. He got to play tailback his junior year. That was 1980, and Marcus played well. He

Marcus started playing tailback in 1980.

Marcus and Coach Robinson pause after football practice.

was second in the nation that year in rushing. He gained 1,563 yards. South Carolina's George Rogers gained 1,781 yards to place first. Despite Marcus' good record, he was considered a failure by many people. USC's former tailback, Charles White, had been the best in the country. People in California expected Marcus to be just as good.

The USC Trojans ended the season with an 8-2-1 record. That was considered a fair year. The team's pass-

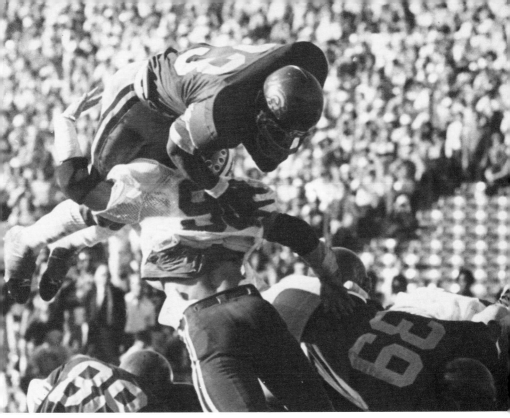

Marcus goes over the top of Washington State's line to score a touchdown.

ing game was off. The Trojans passed for 50 yards per game less than the season before. Worse, Marcus often slipped when he was running with the ball. It seemed like he was always just a step away from breaking for long yardage.

The USC fans forgot that playing tailback was a new position for Marcus. They didn't give him credit for the good job he was doing with so little experience.

THE BEST TAILBACK IN THE NATION

After Marcus' junior year, some sportswriters and alumni of USC told Coach Robinson to replace Marcus at tailback. They wanted a flashier ball carrier. Robinson told everyone to back off. "Next season," he said, "Marcus will be doing things no other back ever did before." Robinson's prediction was correct.

During the summer before the 1981 season, Marcus told one of the USC coaches that he wanted to rush for 2,000 yards his senior year. No other college player had ever rushed for 2,000 yards in a season. Pittsburgh's Tony Dorsett had come as close as anyone. He got 1,948 yards on 338 carries in 1976.

One of the games USC played in 1981 was against Oklahoma. The Sooners were ahead 24-21 late in the game. Marcus had already carried the ball 35 times. He had gained 183 yards. The Trojans handed Marcus the ball on the next four plays. He gained 31 more yards to set up the winning touchdown. "He's better than I thought," said Oklahoma coach, Barry Switzer. "He's probably the best back in the country."

Switzer was right. Marcus Allen had become the best tailback in the nation. Now the big question was whether he could rush for 2,000 yards. He had two games left in the 1981 season. He needed only 32 yards to be the first college player to reach the 2,000 mark. Marcus reached the

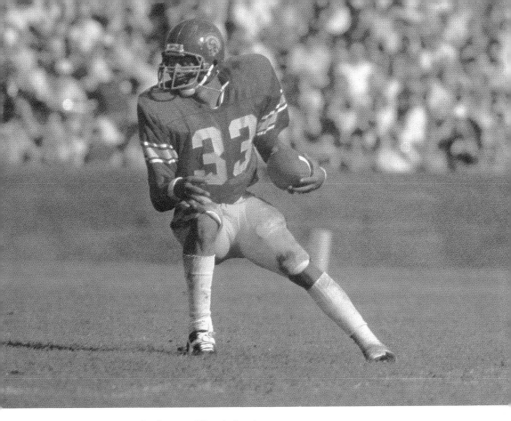

*In 1981, Marcus was the best tailback in the
United States.*

magic number early in the first quarter of the game against
the University of Washington. He rushed for 13 yards on
his fourth carry of the game. That run brought him to
2,000 yards exactly. Three plays later, Marcus cracked
over center for four more yards to move past the 2,000
yard mark. Even the Washington fans cheered Marcus'
performance.

After the game, Marcus was depressed. His team had lost the game and their hopes to play in the Rose Bowl. "What I did doesn't mean all that much right now," he said. "All I'm thinking about is that we didn't win the game."

Marcus got over his depression in a hurry. He ended the 1981 season with fifteen new college football records. For instance, he gained a total of 2,342 yards. That total included yards gained rushing and pass receiving. Marcus had the highest per-game average in a season (212.9 yards). He had the most 200-yard games in a row (five), and the most 200-yard games in a career (eleven). Marcus also led the Trojans in pass receiving, too, his junior and senior years. Such records could not be ignored.

Marcus Allen was also awarded the 1981 Heisman Trophy as the best college football player in the country. He received 441 first-place votes against 152 votes for runner-up Hershel Walker. There was no doubt about it. Marcus Allen had made it big. Why was he so much better than he had been the year before? "I wanted to be," said Allen. The great O. J. Simpson rated him with the best running backs of all time.

The person most thrilled with such a super year was Allen himself. He made appearances all over the country after winning the Heisman. He was on several television specials, as well as *Good Morning America* and the *Today Show.*

Allen was a Public Administration major at USC. He did not graduate, however. He was one semester short of

Marcus Lamarr Allen became the forty-seventh
winner of the Heisman Memorial Trophy.

graduation. "I left school because I won the Heisman Trophy," Allen said. "I did a lot of traveling. And I missed the entire last semester. But I'm going back to school. What's important is that you get your degree."

Today, Allen spends some of his free time talking to young athletes about the importance of getting a college degree. He tells them that sports are important. Everyone can identify with an athlete. But he also tells them that a lot of athletes don't get a degree. They see the glamour in sports, but don't like the hard work that goes along with getting an education. "It's sad but true," says Allen.

ALLEN SIGNS WITH THE RAIDERS

In 1981, Marcus Allen was the best tailback in college football. But scouts for several National Football League (NFL) teams had doubts about Allen's abilities. Some felt he wasn't fast enough for the NFL. Some felt he really wasn't that good. They said anybody could gain yards behind USC's offensive line. The Oakland Raiders let the other teams doubt. They wanted Marcus Allen. But they did not expect to get him. Eight other teams got to pick a player before the Raiders had their first turn in the NFL draft. The Raiders were sure Allen would be picked by the time it was their turn.

In his senior year at USC, Marcus gained 2,342 yards.

Draft day arrived. As expected, New England opened by selecting Ken Sims from Texas. Johnie Cooks, a linebacker from Mississippi State, went to Baltimore. Cleveland grabbed linebacker Chip Banks from USC. Two quarterbacks were next to go—Ohio State's Art Schlichter was drafted by Baltimore, and Brigham Young's Jim McMahone was chosen by Chicago. Seattle then picked Jeff Bryant from Clemson.

Minnesota was next. The Vikings needed a running back. They chose Stanford's Darrin Nelson. When Houston picked Penn State guard, Mike Munchak, only Atlanta stood between the Raiders and Allen. The Falcons took Arizona State's Gerald Riggs. Marcus Allen had not been picked.

The Raiders were shocked when their turn came. They couldn't believe the Heisman Trophy winner was still available. So the Raiders grabbed him. "We didn't figure

The Raiders were surprised when they were able to draft Marcus in the first round.

18

there was any way he would be available," said Ron Wolf who directs the Raiders' scouting. "For our team, Allen was the best player in the draft."

The Raiders signed Allen to a reported four-year, $1.5 million contract.

THE RAIDERS MOVE TO LOS ANGELES

The owners of the Raiders had been trying to move their team from Oakland to Los Angeles. The National Football League did not want the team to move. For three years, the case was bogged down in court. Then, in April of 1982, the Raiders won their case and were finally allowed to move to Los Angeles.

So when Allen signed with the Raiders, they were about to begin their first season in Los Angeles. That created some problems. Los Angeles had been the home of the L.A. Rams for many years. Now there were two NFL teams from the same city. The question was whether there would be enough fans to support both teams. The Raiders faced an uphill battle. They were not exactly welcome in Los Angeles. As the Oakland Raiders, they had come to town twice in the 70's and had beaten the Rams both times.

The Raiders played their first exhibition game of 1982, against the San Francisco 49ers. Allen carried the ball for the first time in his professional career. He gained nine yards. The following week against Detroit, Allen scored a touchdown—he caught a 15-yard pass from quarterback Jim Plunkett. By the third week of exhibition play, Allen was the Raiders' No. 1 halfback.

The Raiders played their first game of the regular season in Los Angeles on September 12, 1982. Thanks to Allen's great debut as a rookie, they upset the defending Super

As a first-year rookie, Allen lost little time in showing the Raiders that they had selected the right man.

Bowl champion, 23-17. Allen got 180 of his team's 255 yards. He rushed for 116 yards on 23 carries. He added 64 more yards on four pass receptions. Allen scored his first

NFL touchdown. "Both teams just hung in there," said Allen. "They made mistakes; we made mistakes. Maybe the difference was in attitude. We wanted to win a little more."

The announcer at Candlestick Park, where the game was played, had a hard time remembering that the Raiders had moved from Oakland. He had to correct himself

several times, after calling the team the "Oakland Raiders." No one had a hard time remembering Marcus Allen. He played like a true champion.

NATIONAL FOOTBALL LEAGUE STRIKE

1982 was a difficult year for professional football. After the first two weeks of the season, all of the players went on strike. It was the first regular-season strike in the league's sixty-three-year history.

The players and team owners had been talking off and on for seven months. One of the things the players wanted was half of the money earned by showing NFL games on television. The team owners rejected that idea. So a strike was called by the players. "No games will be played until the owners deal with the players fairly," said the head of the players' union.

Both sides said they were prepared for the strike. The team owners arranged for bank loans to cover their losses. A strike fund had been set up by the players. They would not get paid by the teams during the strike. "We have enough to hold out for as long as it takes," said Gene Upshaw, one of Allen's teammates.

The NFL strike lasted fifty-seven days. It was the longest, and most costly, strike in sports history. The players did not win the right to any of the money earned by showing NFL games on television. But they got their way on some other things and agreed to go back to work. When it was all over, 112 football games had been canceled. The schedule was set to resume on November 21, 1982. The teams would play a total of nine games for the season, seven games less than they usually played.

Marcus scored two touchdowns in the 1982 game against the San Diego Chargers.

BACK TO BUSINESS

Allen and the Raiders went back to work on November 22. They defeated the San Diego Chargers, 28-24. Allen

played well until a game a few weeks later against the Cincinnati Bengals. Cincinnati held Allen to exactly zero yards in eight attempts. The Raiders' offensive line never got used to the Bengals' defense. Los Angeles suffered its only loss of the shortened season, 31-17. "Marcus Allen?" asked Bengal player Eddie Edwards. "Why, he's just another rookie." Allen took his bad day in stride. "O. J. Simpson told me he once had a game against the Colts where he carried seven times and ended up losing yards," said Allen after the game. "At least I broke even!"

Allen did more than break even in the next game, which was against Seattle. On the Raiders' third play, he raced for 33 yards. Later in the second quarter, he took a pitch-

out at his own 44-yard line. He ran down the field and almost scored a touchdown. Linebacker Bruce Scholtz brought Allen down at the three-yard line. No matter. Allen scored the Raiders' fourth touchdown on the very next play.

The Raiders beat Seattle, 28-23. Allen gained 121 yards on 12 carries in the first half alone. He finished the day with 156 yards and 2 touchdowns. It was his best game yet in the NFL. In five games, Allen had rushed for 415 yards, the third-highest total in the American Football Conference (AFC). He led the AFC with 7 touchdowns.

On December 18, the two Los Angeles teams, the Raiders and the Rams, played each other for the first time in Los Angeles. Sixty-five thousand fans booed and cheered the rivals. It was the first time in the history of the NFL that over $1 million in tickets had been sold!

The Rams fought as if they were playing the Super Bowl. But they lost because of Allen. He ran and dived for an early touchdown. Later, he exploded for six more points. Then, with the Raiders behind, he scored again from the 11-yard line. The Raiders won, 37-31. Allen gained more yards—103—than the entire Rams' backfield!

Allen was playing his rookie year with nerve and guts. He was the exciting runner the Raiders had been looking for. "You can't drag Allen down with one arm," said Seattle player Manu Tuiasosopo. "I know. I had three or four missed tackles. You've got to hold him up and nail him. That guy is remarkable. He just keeps coming at you."

Cincinnati held Marcus to zero yards in their 1982 meeting.

Allen led the AFC with seven touchdowns in 1982.

Allen added depth to the Raiders. He could run, catch, block, and throw. "He's a complete back," said teammate Kenny King. Another teammate, Lester Hayes, said that

Allen was blessed. "When God made O. J. Simpson," said Hayes, "He decided there would be only one clone. And that's Marcus Allen!"

Just like O. J. Simpson, Allen wears jersey number 32.

Allen didn't like being called a Simpson clone. "I'm an individual," he said. Still, it was true that he and Simpson had a lot in common. Both O. J. and Allen were born in California. Both set college rushing records in the same USC position. Both stood six-foot-two and weighed 210 pounds. Each scored 23 touchdowns and 138 points in his senior year at USC. Each won the Heisman Trophy. As a pro, Simpson wore jersey number 32. Allen wears the same number!

Allen may never get enough carries to equal Simpson's record-setting, 2,000-yard season in the NFL. He proved during his rookie year, though, that there are some things he does better than Simpson already. Allen is an excellent blocker. He learned how to block as a sophomore at USC when he played fullback. Allen's blocking made it possible for Charles White to win the Heisman. "I was hurting every week," said Allen. "I'd cry and moan to get out of practice each day. Fortunately, Coach Robinson didn't listen to me."

Allen is a very unselfish player. When teammates see a Heisman Trophy winner go into a game and block the way Allen does, they love it. After every game, the team watches films to see what they did right and wrong. Allen's teammates cheer him as much for his blocking as for his moves. "I think he's as good a blocker as he is a runner," said Guard Curt Marsh.

Allen can catch a pass better than O. J. Simpson, too. He has always had "good hands." He had to have good hands to play quarterback in high school. He also led USC in pass catches his final two seasons. As a running back for the Raiders his first year, Allen caught 38 passes for 401 yards!

Allen also knows how to run. He moves so well that more than one opponent must cover him when he runs with the ball. He has the quickness and the balance to get his work done. Allen's teammates love to talk about his abilities as a runner. They say he is like a greased pig. Allen is hard to grab and even harder to pull down. Marcus Allen finds the hole in the defense and makes things happen. He is exciting!

The Raiders' coaches knew Allen could run. What they

didn't realize was that he could block and catch passes, as well. That is what separates the great running backs from the good ones. There are a lot of good backs in the pros. There are only a few great backs like Marcus Allen.

ROOKIE OF THE YEAR

For a guy who was chosen late in the draft, Allen did a super job his rookie year. He led the Raiders to an 8-1 record, the best in the AFC. In those nine games, Allen rushed for 697 yards. He was good for 5.7 yards every time he touched the ball. He scored 14 touchdowns to lead the NFL. He was the first rookie to lead the league in scoring since Gale Sayers did it for the Chicago Bears in 1965. No other player in the league could match those all-purpose numbers! He was voted Rookie of the Year. "There is no question," said Raiders' coach Tom Flores. "God blessed us by giving us Marcus Allen."

Allen was also voted All-Pro and played on the first-team in the Pro Bowl. Allen gave credit for his awards to his football education at USC. He felt he learned a lot there. "To me, pro football is really not that complicated," said Allen. "Not when you've had such good training." For Allen, pro ball was no different from what he expected. He knew he was going to do well. He was ready for the pressure.

Allen says he was not nervous about playing before the fans. What did awe him was playing against many of his

"To me, pro football is really not that complicated."

childhood heroes. "Just playing against some of the players you've seen on television since you were a kid awed me," he said. "You say 'wow' when you finally get the chance to play with them." Allen had to forget he was playing against men who were ten or eleven years older than he. He had to convince himself he was just as good as they were. That is exactly what he did. If anyone doubted his talents before he turned pro, nobody questioned his playing now.

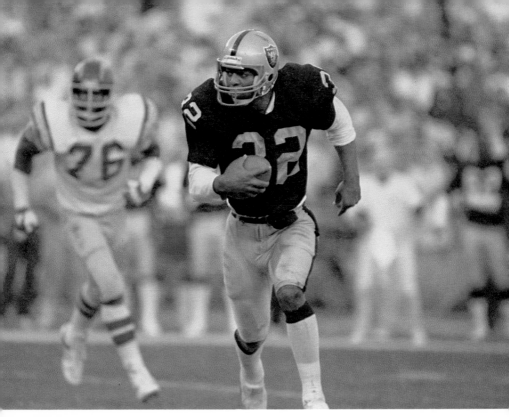

During the 1983 season, Marcus had only one
100-yard game.

ALLEN'S SECOND YEAR IN THE PROS

Things did not go so well for Allen his second year with the Raiders. Every time he got the ball, the defense surrounded him. Allen tried to battle his way through the defense. He just wasn't gaining big yardage. By the end of October, he had only one 100-yard game. That was against Miami. A year before, he already had three 100-yard games and had run for 11 touchdowns. Now he had only two.

Reporters started asking Allen what was wrong. "I don't care," he said. "We're winning, that's what's important. It's just personally frustrating." Allen's coaches said they were not worried about him. He had missed one-and-a-half games because of a hip injury. They thought he might be playing more carefully. The coaches also said that he just needed to be patient.

Allen tried to keep his spirits up. He tried to remember that it is very hard to stay the best. "Things will get better," he explained. Allen thought that he might have worked too hard during the winter and spring. He was tired, he said.

The Raiders made it to the play-offs, but Allen's second season was a letdown. He averaged only 3.8 yards per carry. He had only one 100-yard game. His longest gain was only 19 yards. But he looked forward to the play-offs. Perhaps his luck would change.

ON THE WAY TO THE SUPER BOWL

The Raiders played the Pittsburgh Steelers in the first round of the play-offs. What a time for Allen to start looking like himself again! He gained 121 yards on 13 carries. That included a 49-yard run. He set a Raider record of

9.3 yards per carry. He also had two touchdowns. The Raiders won, 38-10.

The Raiders met the Seattle Seahawks to decide the AFC championship. Allen continued to play great football. He put on his best performance as a Raider. From the start, the ball was in his hands. The Raiders' Lester Hayes intercepted a Seahawk pass on the first series of the game. That put the ball on the Seattle 27-yard line. Allen ran the first four plays and set up a Raider field goal. By halftime, he had rushed for 70 yards. In the third quarter, Jim Plunkett handed off to Allen. He raced 43 yards to the Seattle 3. "If I hadn't slipped, I would have gone in," he said. On the next down, Allen caught a pass for a touchdown.

In the fourth quarter, Allen fumbled a pitch out from Plunkett. It was his only fumble of the game and it didn't really matter in the end. The Raiders beat Seattle, 30-14. Allen had run the ball 25 times for 154 yards. He picked up another 62 yards on seven pass catches. "I played okay," he said after the game. "A few times I missed blitzes I should have picked up on. Other than that, I did okay."

Allen was tired and aching after the game. Someone had stuck an elbow in his face mask as he was blocking for Frank Hawkins. "Wasn't much of a good block either!" Allen said. Despite the injury, Allen had played his best game as a Raider. His team was headed for the Super Bowl!

*Marcus played his best game as a Raider in the
AFC championship game with the Seattle
Seahawks.*

THE SUPER BOWL

The Raiders were going to meet the Washington Redskins in Super Bowl XVIII. Sportswriters and players

Marcus arrives for practice before Super Bowl XVIII.

thought the game would be the meanest Super Bowl ever. "The Raiders will talk to us on the field," said Redskin tackle Joe Jacoby. "They'll try to psych us out. They'll push and shove after the play is over. The Redskins will take that kind of treatment personally.''

Because of a hip injury, Marcus had missed the regular season game with the Redskins.

The Raiders and Redskins had played in the fifth week of the regular season. The Redskins had won, 37-35. Many said it had been the best game of the season. The Raiders

Marcus practices blocking before the Super Bowl game against the Redskins.

played that game without Allen. A hip injury had caused him to miss the game.

But Allen did play in Super Bowl XVIII. He showed the

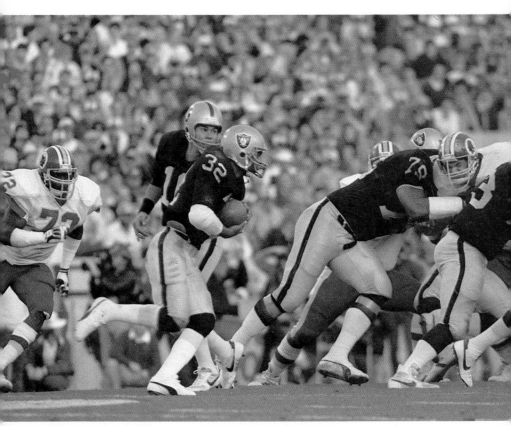

Marcus gained fifty-one yards in the first half of Super Bowl XVIII.

world that he was the best back the Raiders have ever had.

Allen started off slowly. At halftime he had 51 yards on 11 carries. In the third quarter, though, he showed the

Redskins his stuff. Early in the quarter, on second and goal, Allen ran right, cut back left and slid into the end zone. At the end of the third quarter, the Raiders took

Marcus runs around right end.

over at their own 26-yard line. Allen was handed the ball. He swept to his left where he was shut off by Ken Coffey. Then he changed directions. Allen ran inside, straight up

Holding the ball in one hand, Allen scoots by a Redskin defender.

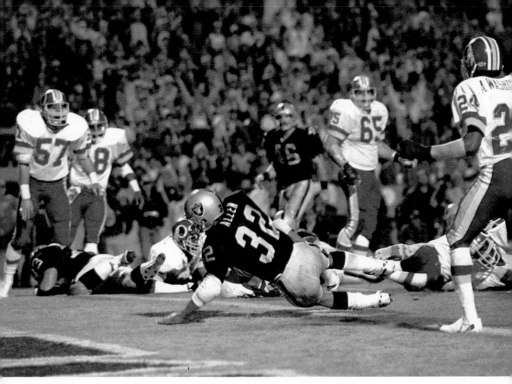

Marcus scores one of his Super Bowl XVIII touchdowns.

the middle of the field. He ran past linebackers Monte
Coleman and Rich Milot. He ran past middle linebacker
Neal Olkewicz, who fell down. He ran away from corner-
back Anthony Washington to score a seventy-four yard
touchdown. That made the score 35-9 in favor of the
Raiders. "They overpursued," said Allen later. "I kind of
cut back, they kind of missed me. It was all reaction. No
thinking involved."

"I was just picking myself up off the ground," Raider
right guard, Mickey Marvin, said. "Then I looked around
and a rocket went through!"

On his 20 carries in the game, Allen ended up with 191

yards. He broke the Super Bowl rushing record set by John Riggins of the Redskins the previous year. He added two more Super Bowl records. Marcus had the longest run—his 74-yarder. And he had gained the most overall yards—209. That included the two passes he caught for 18 yards.

Allen had not had a 100-yard game during the last thirteen weeks of the regular season. He had three in a row in the playoffs! He finished the post-season with 466 yards on 58 carries. That figures out to be eight yards a carry. He also had 14 pass receptions and 5 touchdowns.

"I learned a lot this year," Allen said after the game. "I learned patience. I was trying too hard earlier in the season to make things happen. That's how I got in trouble with fumbles and mental errors. But Coach Flores never gave up on me and I'm grateful.

"I felt like I could run all day today. I didn't know I set a record until I saw it on the scoreboard. My teammates were congratulating me. You dream of moments like this, but you never think they'll happen.

"But the best thing was seeing the smiles on my parents' faces. I found my mother on the field after the game and gave her a big kiss. She had tears in her eyes. If I can give my parents this moment, that's my Super Bowl."

Allen was awarded the Most Valuable Player award for Super Bowl XVIII. He gave credit to his "bunch of crazy teammates." In fact, he said if he had to vote, he would have chosen Reggie Kinlaw, defensive tackle for the Raiders. Allen said he wouldn't want to play with any other team.

"What's left to accomplish?" Allen asked. "I've been a Heisman Trophy winner. I've played in the Rose Bowl. And now I'm the Super Bowl MVP. I'm not greedy, but I'm still hungry. I want more."

THE FUTURE

Marcus Allen is attractive and a fairly good speaker. Maybe he will take up acting when his football career is over. "Oh, I think it would be great fun to get into acting," Allen says. "But it's not solid and steady." He also notes that there aren't a lot of roles for black actors. What he'd like to do after football is broadcasting or sportscasting. "I'm going to work very hard at it," he says.

Allen knows he will have to work with a speech coach to improve his speaking abilities. He has watched other athletes go into broadcasting. It is hard work. Allen feels comfortable, however, with his ability to communicate. He expresses himself well. He has an image of being honest and a gentleman. Those are good qualities for a broadcaster.

Allen also wants to do whatever is possible to help each member of his family reach their goals. He feels they have helped him succeed. He wants to do the same for each of them.

For now, football remains Allen's big love. He looks forward to his third year as a pro with the Raiders. After his outstanding post-season play, he feels he is back in the groove.

Marcus with the trophy he got for being the Most Valuable Player in Super Bowl XVIII.

Marcus Allen has high standards. He expects more from himself than any of his fans, coaches, or teammates. He is a great athlete, with the ability to put a fair season under his belt and come back fighting. Marcus Allen never loses confidence in himself. That has been the key to his success. As the Raiders' team owner, Al Davis, says, "He's everything you always dream about in a professional football player!"

MARCUS ALLEN'S PROFESSIONAL STATISTICS

1982* NFL

	No.	Yards	Average	Touchdowns
Rushing	160	697	4.4	11
Receiving	38	401	10.6	3

	Att.	Comp.	Yards	Touchdowns
Passing	4	1	47	0

Total Points   84

1983 NFL

	No.	Yards	Average	Touchdowns
Rushing	266	1014	3.8	9
Receiving	68	590	8.7	2

	Att.	Comp.	Yards	Touchdowns
Passing	7	4	111	3

Total Points   72

*8-game season due to NFL strike.